High Days
& Holy Days

WORSHIP RESOURCES FOR THE LITURGICAL YEAR

Michael Forster

Kevin Mayhew

First published in 1993 by
KEVIN MAYHEW LTD
Rattlesden
Bury St Edmunds
Suffolk IP30 0SZ

The publishers wish to express their gratitude
to the following:

Inter-Varsity Press for *Jesus of the Scars* by Edward Shillito,
published after World War 1, and quoted by William Temple
in his *Readings in St John's Gospel*, pp. 384-385.

Kingsway Publications for *A Litany of the Resurrection* by Ian Bunting
from *Prayers for Today's Church* by Dick Williams.

Robson Books for *I have a dream*
from *The Words of Martin Luther King* by Coretta Scott King.

The Division of Christian Education
of the National Council of the Churches of Christ in the USA
for extracts from the *New Revised Standard Version of the Bible*, copyright 1989.

ISBN 086209 386 4

Front Cover: *Angel playing the Lute* by Rosso Florentino (1494-1540).
Galleria Degli Uffizi, Florence/Bridgeman Art Library, London.
Reproduced by kind permission.

Typesetting & Page Creation by Anne Haskell
Cover Design by Graham Johnstone
Printed and bound in Great Britain.

CONTENTS

FOREWORD

THESE services are intended as a resource for anyone responsible for leading worship on special occasions in the christian year. They can be used in a variety of ways.

The Advent and Lent ceremonies are designed to be slotted into the weekly worship in those seasons. The ones in this book use the lectionary themes from Year One ASB. Careful thought will be needed as to how they may best be fitted into the service.

The other services are complete in themselves, and are not connected specifically with the lectionary. They do not, of course, need to be used as complete services, but could be 'dipped into' by ministers and others designing their own services; or they could simply be used to spark off ideas. However, they can be used as they stand with the minimum of adaptation. The main preparation required will be in the briefing of readers for the various parts.

All the orders were prepared for use in a specific situation. Most of them included sermons, which have been replaced with scripted dialogues. This makes the services easily usable, especially in those churches without their own ministers. Of course, sermons can easily be substituted if desired. I hope that the material will be used flexibly and in widely varied ways, according to particular needs and traditions

Except for the Easter service, the patterns are all non-eucharistic. There is no particular reason for this – it just happens to be the case. However, there is no reason why a form of eucharist cannot be interpolated, where it is felt appropriate; again, flexibility is the word.

Hymns are suggested, with alternatives, but again local circumstances may well require that these are changed. Some of the hymns have been specially written, and these are included in an appendix. The others are generally available in various hymn books.

Finally, liturgical patterns can be excellent servants but intolerable masters! No doubt these ones are open to a variety of modifications and improvements; the important thing is that the worship offered is as meaningful and worthy as it may be.

MICHAEL FORSTER

ADVENT CANDLE CEREMONIES

Grace Comes With Judgment

ADVENT is a time for preparation, which offers great opportunities. Like any great event, the Christmas celebrations will be all the better if adequately prepared, and that means by the whole church. These ceremonies offer a way of doing just that. They are intended to be slotted into the normal Sunday service, with whatever adjustments may be necessary to the usual format.

Each week's ceremony consists of readings and dialogue, ending with the Advent Carol. One verse of this is sung on Advent Sunday, two on Advent Two, and so on until the whole carol is sung on Christmas Day.

The aim is to see the wholeness of the Christmas story, not only as hope but as challenge. Of course, it is good news, but it calls us to decisions and actions which we may find very difficult and costly, if we are really to accept it. In this, the questioning attitude of Voice 1 plays a vital part. It is important not to caricature this role – such voices are needed in the church to prod others of us to think our faith through more carefully.

The readings are from the ASB lectionary, Year 1

An Advent Crown of five candles will need to be prepared in advance.

ADVENT SUNDAY

Reader	Hear the word of God. Isaiah 52: 7-10
Voice 1	Well, it's all very nice, isn't it – but is it true? To listen to that, you'd think all we have to do is leave it to God, and everything's going to be hunky-dory! I'm not sure it's that simple.
Voice 2	No, it's not that simple. But in the end, the gospel is about hope or it's about nothing. We're just proclaiming the hope that is in us.
Voice 1	But if it's such good news, why is it that most people just don't seem to want to hear it?
Voice 2	Well, it's not just good news – there's always another side to anything. Take the freeing of slaves, for example . . .
Voice 1	That's good news.
Voice 2	If you're a slave – but not if you own one.
Voice 1	I see what you mean – one man's meat . . .
Voice 2	. . . is another man's poison – or woman's if it comes to that!
Voice 1	So, for some people, the gospel's good news, and they welcome it . . .
Voice 2	. . . while for others, it's bad news, and they oppose it.
Voice 1	One person's grace is another person's judgment.
Reader	Hear the gospel of Christ. Luke 21: 25-33
	A child lights the first candle.
Minister	We sing the first verse of the Advent Carol, Hear the prophet calling. (See Appendix)

SECOND SUNDAY IN ADVENT

Voice 1   What are we thinking about today, then?

Voice 2   The word of God in the Old Testament.

Voice 1   Why do we have to bother with that?
              The New Testament's our book, isn't it?

Voice 2   The New Testament's very important, but you can't just ignore
              the Old. After all, that was the bible Jesus knew – so if we're trying
              to understand his ideas it helps to read his bible.

Reader   Hear the word of God.
              Isaiah 55:1-11

Voice 1   That was very nice – what was it about?

Voice 2   Basically, about God longing to give good things to his people.

Voice 1   Well if he's longing to, why doesn't he just get on and do it?

Voice 2   Because they won't let him. The trouble is that their ideas
              about what are good things are not always the same as God's –
              so what he wants to give them, they don't want.

Voice 1   How d'you mean?

Voice 2   Well, for instance, what would you rather have, ten thousand pounds,
              or my friendship?

Voice 1   I wish you hadn't asked me that . . .

Voice 2   Exactly – and while God's trying to give his people the things he
              knows are good for them, they don't want to know,
              because they're too busy chasing their own ideas.

Voice 1   Why do you keep saying 'they'?

Voice 2   Oh, all right then – 'We'!

Reader   Hear the gospel of Christ.
              John 5:36-47

              A child lights two candles.

Minister   We sing the first two verses of the Advent Carol,
              Hear the prophet calling. (See Appendix)

Reader	Hear the word of God. Isaiah 40:1-11
Voice 2	Well, there's the message: 'Prepare'. That's what Advent's about – preparing for Christmas.
Voice 1	Oh yes, and don't I know it – presents to buy, decorations to put up . . .
Voice 2	That's not what I mean – I mean preparing ourselves.
Voice 1	In what way?
Voice 2	Well, imagine you were moving house.
Voice 1	Don't talk to me about moving house! Last time we moved house, we were amazed at the rubbish we'd collected.
Voice 2	Exactly. So, if God came and called you on a journey, would you be ready, or would you have to leave a lot of precious things behind?
Voice 1	You mean like my digital Nicam stereo television with a flatter, squarer screen and built-in video recorder?
Voice 2	Quite probably, along with a pretty precious load of prejudices and insecurities.
Voice 1	D'you think you could arrange for God to wait a little longer?
Voice 2	That's the point. The Good News is that God wants to set us free. The bad news is that he wants to do it now – and what he wants to free us from are the things we want to cling onto. It' s a case of . . .
Voice 1	I know – grace and judgment. Grace if you want to go on the journey – judgment if you want to take all your possessions and prejudices with you.
Voice 2	That's about it. And that's why, when John the Baptist proclaimed the same message, he got a bit of opposition.
Reader	Hear the gospel of Christ. John 1:19-28
	A child lights three candles.
Minister	We sing the first three verses of the Advent Carol, Hear the prophet calling. (See Appendix)

Fourth Sunday in Advent

Reader	Hear the word of God. Isaiah 11:1-9
Voice 1	So, we're in for a bit of wise counsel, are we? A bit of good government. Some people would say that the world's been waiting a long time for that!
Voice 2	So had the Israelites. The royal house of David had become corrupt and lost power, and there'd been a pretty horrific period of injustice, following it. So they were ready for some good news.
Voice 1	But it's rather odd stuff, isn't it?
Voice 2	Sounds reasonable to me – good government will bring peace and justice.
Voice 1	Oh yes, that's all fair enough. It's the next bit I find difficult – I mean, in the real world, lions don't eat straw and leopards don't lie down with kids. I suppose it might happen, but I don't think the kid would get much sleep.
Voice 2	I suppose you would also say that in the real world, virgins don't have children and gods don't become human!
Voice 1	Now what are you getting at?
Reader	Hear the gospel of Christ. Luke 1: 26 -38a
Voice 1	All right, point taken! So what's the connection?
Voice 2	With what?
Voice 1	With grace and judgment. I can see the grace – it's obvious – but what's the judgment?
Voice 2	Well firstly, not everyone wants the world to be like that. And if it's going to be, we're all going to have to make sacrifices.
Voice 1	And secondly?
Voice 2	Secondly, the whole emphasis is on unexpected things – as you yourself pointed out. We like to think we understand exactly how the world works – that everything's predictable.
Voice 1	Except the weather!
Voice 2	Except the weather. But these passages say that we can't be so sure. God's quite likely to do something we don't expect and to prove us wrong about all the things we thought we knew.
Voice 1	Now there's an uncomfortable idea!
	A child lights four candles.
Minister	We sing the first four verses of the Advent Carol, Hear the prophet calling. (See Appendix)

CHRISTMAS DAY

Reader	Hear the word of God. Isaiah 62: 1-5
Voice 1	Terrific! We're all going to live happily ever after.
Voice 2	Yes, there's some truth in that – but it's not that simple
Voice 1	I might have known that where you're concerned, nothing could be that simple!
Voice 2	Saint Augustine once said a prayer that's become famous. he said, 'O God, make me pure, but not yet!' We all want a wonderful world, but the trouble is that we also rather enjoy some of the things that are wrong with this one.
Voice 1	Such as what?
Voice 2	Our priorities, for a start. We want to carry on thinking that certain kinds of things, or people, are important, while God's trying to tell us something very different.
Voice 1	Give me an example.
Voice 2	O.K. Put it this way: if you were told that God had come to earth, where would you look for him?
Voice 1	I suppose in a church or perhaps a palace.
Voice 2	You wouldn't look in a stable?
Voice 1	Don't be silly!
Voice 2	And who would you expect to be the first to know about it?
Voice 1	I suppose the local clergyman – except that he's normally the last to know anything, and even then he forgets!
Voice 2	But you wouldn't expect God to go and tell the night watchman at Marconi's?[1]
Voice 1	Now you really *are* being silly!
Reader	Hear the gospel of Christ. Luke 2: 1-14 *A child lights all five candles.*
Minister	We sing the Advent Carol, Hear the prophet calling. (See Appendix)

[1]Here insert the name of a well-known local company.

NATIVITY SERVICE

MANY people come to Nativity services, for a variety of reasons, and with different degrees of openness. A considerable number find it hard to accept anything other than the traditional and unchallenging – even unrealistic – production. This service uses the expected medium, but includes other material to try and help people move forward a step or two toward an understanding of the incarnation which makes more contact with present-day life.

The basic format is a fairly traditional series of readings and carols. During the readings, the children can mime the Christmas story in the usual way.

The opening dialogue links in with the Advent Candle Ceremony. It is not exactly the same, however, since many people may be present who have not been at the Advent services. Then come the readings and carols, interspersed with which are some interviews. It would appear that the local radio station has used the newly-discovered wonder of time-travel to go back and get an innkeeper's view of the event.

ORDER OF SERVICE

WELCOME

Welcome to this special nativity service. A special welcome to visitors – we hope you enjoy worshipping with us. Of course we're not quite at Christmas, yet – which is good news for those of us who are nowhere near ready for it! – so after the first hymn and prayer, we're going to hear a dialogue which is not about Christmas itself, but about preparing for it. Then we shall begin the traditional series of readings and Christmas carols, combined with an acting out of the story. But there's a difference. We're a very scientific crowd here, and we're proud to announce that we have mastered time-travel. So we're sending our own reporter – from Radio Buckminster[2] – back to the scene to interview one of the important characters in the story, and get her view of it. But we begin with the first hymn.

HYMN   Hark the glad sound
            or O come, O come, Emmanuel

OPENING PRAYER

Eternal God, we come to celebrate your presence in the world; your eternal presence made explicit in Jesus. We come to wonder at the simplicity and innocence, to enjoy the familiar story and the memories it evokes. We come to join in the traditional celebrations of Christmas, and for many other reasons as well. We pray that as we do all that, you will open our hearts to the challenge of this story. Help us to see ourselves in your story and you in ours. Draw us to this familiar and attractive manger scene where we may worship you; send us out to find you in the mangers of this present world where we may serve you. May we become more aware of your presence among those the world brushes aside, and more open to the voices of apparently insignificant people, who are calling us to hear their story and recognise hope. Loving God, you open yourself to us in Jesus; help us to open ourselves to you. Amen.

READING   Isaiah 40:1-11

DIALOGUE

Voice 2	Well, there's the message: 'Prepare'. That's what Advent's about – preparing for Christmas.
Voice 1	Oh yes, and don't I know it – presents to buy, decorations to put up . . .
Voice 2	That's not what I mean – I mean preparing ourselves
Voice 1	In what way?
Voice 2	Well, imagine you were moving house.
Voice 1	Don't talk to me about moving house! Last time we moved house, it took us about a year to get over it.

[2]Here insert an appropriate local-sounding name

Voice 2	But how did you feel when you were getting ready for it?
Voice 1	Mixed, really - we were very excited about the adventure . . .
Voice 2	But?
Voice 1	But we didn't like leaving the old familiar places and people behind – and we weren't really sure what was ahead.
Voice 2	So, you might have said it was a matter of good news and bad news both at the same time.
Voice 1	Yes, actually that's not a bad way of putting it.
Voice 2	Same with Christmas. God coming into the world is good news in some ways, but bad news in others.
Voice 1	Why?
Voice 2	Well, obviously the world can never be the same again. And although we welcome some kinds of change, we're afraid of others. For example, would you like the world to be simpler, and life to be less hectic?
Voice 1	That's easy – of course I would.
Voice 2	But do you want have less spare cash, an older car, and do without the video-player?
Voice 1	Hmm . . . I see what you mean. Good news and bad news at the same time.
Voice 2	That's right - the bible calls it grace and judgment, but basically that's what it's about.

HYMN   Hear the prophet calling (See Appendix)
or On Jordan's bank

READING   Luke 1:26-38

COMMENT

Well, it's not hard to imagine that Mary was pretty surprised by all that. What amazed her most of all, though was that God had chosen *her*. She didn't regard herself as important. Come to that, nobody regarded her as important – except Joseph, of course, and perhaps his and her parents – but the rest of the world didn't know she existed. Why her? We can get an indication of how surprised she was from the way she broke the news to Elizabeth.

READING   Luke 1: 46-56

CAROL   Born in the night
or A great and mighty wonder

READING   Luke 2:1-7

COMMENT

Now there's someone who wasn't prepared. The most important family in history were there on the doorstep, and the innkeeper hadn't got room. I suppose if they'd looked important, some room would have been made –

we always make room for the really important people and things. But our sense of values is not usually the same as God's. Let's hear what the innkeeper has to say to Radio Buckminster's[3] reporter at the scene.

Interviewer   Hello, I've come to Bethlehem. And if you're thinking of coming here, forget it, unless you like sleeping rough. All the hotels and guest houses are full to bursting! It's so bad that I've even heard a rumour of a young couple who are having to sleep in the stable – and that would be bad enough, but their first child has been born here, and the only cradle they could find for him was the manger of hay provided for the animals. Rachel[4], you're the licensee of this hotel. Doesn't it worry you that this situation has arisen?

Rachel   Well, I'm sorry for them of course, but you've got to see it from my angle. The town's full of people with nowhere to go. They don't bother to book in advance – just turn up out of the blue, and then I get the blame when they've nowhere to stay.

Interviewer   Yes, but surely, in the case of a pregnant woman you could have found something better?

Rachel   It's not my fault she's pregnant – people should organise their lives better. She's not my responsibility.

Interviewer   Well, there's a rumour going around that this is no ordinary family. We've heard stories of people seeing strange visions, and all kinds of things. D'you think it's possible that this is a particularly important family, who are living in your stable?

Rachel   Important? Important? It's just a village carpenter and his wife. You should have seen them when they knocked on my door – anyone less important-looking it's hard to imagine! We get them all here, you know: politicians, entertainers, company directors . . . I know important people when I see them – and take it from me, these are not important.

CAROL   O little town
or Let all mortal flesh keep silence

READING   Luke 2:8-18

Interviewer   Since our last conversation, there have been some further developments. This homeless family have had some visitors. Tell me, Rachel, what do you think about this?

Rachel   Well, since you ask, I'm very glad now that I put them in the stable, and not in the hotel.

Interviewer   Why do you say that?

[3]Again, insert some suitable local-sounding name

[4]Because the Guides presented this, we had a woman innkeeper. This, of course, is no more biblical than the character, and can be changed if necessary!

Rachel Just look at who the visitors are – shepherds! They come in here, straight from the fields, in the clothes they work in, and their sandals covered in mud, and they probably haven't washed since last Passover!

Interviewer But what about this story they tell, about angels saying this baby is a future king?

Rachel Now, be realistic! If God was going to do something like that, don't you think he'd have chosen some more impressive visitors? The priests haven't been to pay their respects, have they? Just a bunch of down-at-heel shepherds!

CAROL In the bleak midwinter
  or It came upon the midnight clear

READING Matthew 2: 1-12

Interviewer This family really does seem to be arousing some interest. Rachel, what about these latest visitors? They're certainly more impressive than the shepherds.

Rachel As far as I can see, they're a bunch of foreign fortune-tellers. They say that King Herod doesn't know anything about this - and if God was going to send a new king, you'd think Herod would be the first to be told, out of courtesy if nothing else.

Interviewer Well, they seem very certain; they've been following the star for a long time.

Rachel Yes, and that says it all – following a star! They're foreigners, and they're pagans. They don't even worship the proper God. How could they know anything? Look, I've got important things to do – I've got a business to run. There's nothing important happening here, and that's it. You just wait – history will show who's right.

CAROL The first Nowell
  or Unto us a boy is born

INTERCESSIONS

 Special prayers particularly for the homeless and the unwanted, and for ourselves in our prejudice and greed.

 We pray with Mary and Joseph
  for all who are made homeless by the policies of governments and the indifference of others

  for all who struggle to bring hope to birth in conditions of poverty, oppression and fear

  for all who confront the value systems of this world

 We pray with the shepherds
  for all who work unsocial hours, or in poor conditions, or whose work is considered by others to be menial

15

for all who are considered insignificant or even repulsive by 'respectable' society

for all who confront the value systems of this world

We pray with the wise men

for all who search the earth and the universe for truth

for all who offer their wealth in your service

for all who speak from outside our traditions, and tell us of your unseen presence among us

for all who confront the value systems of this world

We pray with the innkeeper

for all who are so caught up in the commerce of this world that they fail to recognise you

for all who exploit the poor and vulnerable,
that they might find real life in you

for ourselves, comfortable in our prejudices, secure in our stereotypes; come, God in the poor, God in the homeless, God in the outsider, God in the disreputable, challenge our assumptions, disturb our certainties, question our values, turn our world upside down.
Even so, come, Lord Jesus. Amen.

OFFERING *This could go to some appropriate charity such as Shelter.*

CAROL O come all ye faithful

BENEDICTION

LENT VIGIL CEREMONIES

Christic is in Us, the Hope of Glory

Lent, like Advent, is a time of preparation for a great festival. So it seems appropriate to adapt the Advent ideas for this season. As with Advent, the Lent ceremonies, which fit with the readings in the ASB lectionary (Year One), are not complete in themselves, but are designed to be fitted into the normal order of service, which may need to be slightly adapted. The material has been arranged as suits the occasion, from week to week. Sometimes both readings are used, and sometimes only one. Careful preparation of the whole service will be needed, to make the best use of these ceremonies.

The atmosphere in Lent needs to be a little different, and so the word 'vigil' has been used. The candle may symbolise the watchman's fire as we obey Christ's injunction to the disciples to watch and pray with him.

As in Advent, the questioning role of one of the voices needs to be taken seriously .

Lent is, of course, a penitential season, and a time of self-examination. However, this must not become oppressive and there is a deliberately light-hearted note to these ceremonies which, hopefully, will enable the serious points to be made more effectively. In any case, penitence must always be kept in the context of hope, or it becomes destructively negative. Without hope, what is the point of trying to change?

First Sunday in Lent

Reader	Hear the word of God. Hebrews 2: 14-18
Voice 1	Why's the gospel always on about sin?
Voice 2	Actually, it's always on about hope.
Voice 1	Then why does it say so much about sin?
Voice 2	Because of hope!
Voice 1	I wonder whether I dare ask you to explain that?
Voice 2	I'll try. Suppose I told you that one day the world will be a wonderful place, full of love and peace, no injustice, no hunger, no suffering . . .
Voice 1	I'd ask why, if it can be like that, it's so dreadful now.
Voice 2	Exactly. So the hope – the possibility – shows up all that's wrong in the present.
Voice 1	I think I understand– a bit like reading an ideal home magazine in a room that's dismal and full of cobwebs.
Voice 2	That's about it. We believe that Jesus has shown us what it means to be really human – fully alive.
Voice 1	And that just shows up how un-human we actually are – but there's no hope in that, is there?
Voice 2	Yes there is – because Jesus shows us what is possible – what we all could be.
Voice 1	That's easy to say, but he was special wasn't he? It's harder for us.
Voice 2	The bible says that he was fully human - he was tempted in all the same ways that we are.
Voice 1	So he's a kind of good example?
Voice 2	Partly, but we're also taught that, in a mysterious way, his life is in us. So we don't need to depend just on ourselves.
Voice 1	Well, thank God for that!
	A child lights the candle.
Minister	This is the mystery we proclaim: Christ in us, the hope of glory!
All	Thanks be to God. Amen
Minister	We sing the first verse of the Vigil Hymn. (See Appendix)

Second Sunday in Lent

Reader	Hear the word of God. 1 John 4: 1-6
Voice 1	What was that about?
Voice 2	Discernment.
Voice 1	What ernment?
Voice 2	(Patiently) Not *this* ernment – *dis*cernment – knowing right from wrong.
Voice 1	That's easy!
Voice 2	Is it?
Voice 1	Well, we've got the ten commandments, haven't we?
Voice 2	And what do they say about closing down coal mines?[5]
Voice 1	Pardon?
Voice 2	You say that knowing right from wrong is easy, because of the ten commandments. So, was it right to close all those coal mines? Or, on a more individual level, should you buy South African oranges?[6]
Voice 1	That's not fair – there's nothing about that in the ten commandments.
Voice 2	Nor anywhere else in the bible, if it comes to that, but the bible does give a little help.
Voice 1	How does it do that?
Voice 2	It tells us to test all things by the spirit of Jesus.
Voice 1	What does that mean?
Voice 2	Imagine you're Jesus, and try to think his way – using his ideals, his priorities, and see what you think he would say.
Voice 1	And that makes it easy?
Voice 2	No. It's not a magic formula – we'll still get it wrong sometimes, and probably argue like mad about it, but that's part of the testing process.
Voice 1	And what if we *still* get it wrong?
Voice 2	As I said last week, it doesn't finally depend only on us, anyway. We should do our very best make the right decisions – the decisions we think Jesus would have made. If we get it right, we're a little closer to how he wants things to be.
Voice 1	And if we don't?
Voice 2	If we don't then he and we – and perhaps others as well – will have to live with the consequences. But because his life is in us, there will always be the hope of redeeming the situation.
Voice 1	Well, thank God for that!
	A child lights the candle.
Minister	This is the mystery we proclaim: Christ in us, the hope of glory!
All	Thanks be to God. Amen.
Minister	We sing the first two verses of the Vigil Hymn. (See Appendix)

[5]Here, any appropriate contemporary issue may be used instead. [6]Likewise

THIRD SUNDAY IN LENT

Reader	Hear the word of God. Colossians 1: 24-29
Voice 1	Oh! That old chestnut again!
Voice 2	What old chestnut?
Voice 1	'Rejoicing in suffering'. I suppose it's the desire to have it both ways – to square all the talk of joy with the reality that actually the world's pretty grim, and christians still get tortured and killed. But it's interesting that most people I hear talking about 'rejoicing in suffering' are pretty comfortable. It's easy for them to talk !
Voice 2	I suppose it depends whether the suffering has any purpose to it or not.
Voice 1	How do you mean?
Voice 2	Well, for instance, the pain of childbirth. No-one with any sense denies that it's painful, but usually there's something pretty wonderful at the end of it.
Voice 1	I think I see what you mean. But that only applies to women, and not to all of them, and not all the time.
Voice 2	Yes, but the image is useful. Around the world, a lot of people have chosen to take risks, and to face pain, because they believe there is hope of something worthwhile.
Voice 1	Such as?
Voice 2	I suppose Terry Waite's a very famous example, but there are countless others, and a lot of them will never be famous at all.
Voice 1	You mean, in the 'Third World'?
Voice 2	Yes, but not only there. Take the Corrymeela Community in Northern Ireland, for example – they take the risk of working for peace. It's very painful work, but they think there's a kind of birth at the end of it. And in English cities, where there's tension and sometimes dreadful conflict, people choose to live and work – for the same reason.
Voice 1	All very good, but what's it specifically got to do with Christianity?
Voice 2	We believe that's part of what the cross was about. God, in Jesus, chose to come and live in the world, to accept the pain and to turn it to good.
Voice 1	So where does that leave us?
Voice 2	Following Jesus! We're called to take the same risks – probably in very small ways – where we are. And the promise is that through the risk and pain we experience, we shall find new life.
Voice 1	A bit like having a baby.

Voice 2	Yes, but I haven't finished yet. Let's not forget the *really* good news – it doesn't depend on us alone. We believe that we have the life of Christ actually within us, giving us strength and hope.
Voice 1	Well, thank God for that!
Reader	Hear the gospel of Christ. Luke 9:18-27
	A child lights the candle.
Minister	This is the mystery we proclaim: Christ in us, the hope of glory!
All	Thanks be to God. Amen
Minister	We sing the first three verses of the Vigil Hymn. (See Appendix)

Fourth Sunday in Lent

Reader	Hear the word of God. 2 Corinthians 3:4-18
Voice 1	I'm lost! Does the bible really need to be so complicated?
Voice 2	I must admit, that passage does seem to weave its way around, rather. Basically, what St. Paul is saying is that we can reflect the glory of God in ourselves.
Voice 1	(Cynically) Oh, yes – I know someone like that – goes around wearing a silly grin all the time and saying how wonderful God is – but nobody takes him seriously.
Voice 2	That's not what I'm talking about – and it's not what St. Paul meant, either. Shortly after that passage, he goes on to talk about 'carrying the death of Christ within us'.
Voice 1	That sounds a bit grim!
Voice 2	The point is that we show the glory of God in our openness to others; an openness which can be costly – and painful.
Voice 1	So why do it?
Voice 2	Because God's true glory is found in his relationships with people – and therefore in ours. And you can't have relationships without openness, and you can't have openness without at least the risk of pain.
Voice 1	(Insistently) So why do it?
Voice 2	Because that's how God is working in the world: opening himself up to people, trying to build relationships with us, and taking the pain that that involves – and in all that bringing about true glory in creation.
Reader	Hear the gospel of Christ. Luke 9:28-36
Voice 1	Well, there was a lot about glory there, but where was the pain?
Voice 2	You weren't listening! Luke told us that Jesus was speaking with Elijah and Moses about his suffering.
Voice 1	Why Elijah and Moses?
Voice 2	They represent the Law and the Prophets. We're being shown that what Jesus did was consistent with the Old Testament scriptures.
Voice 1	Why?
Voice 2	Because that shows that it's all in line with God's purpose. Jesus' suffering – his openness – will have a transforming effect, and lead to the true glory of the whole of creation.
Voice 1	So we're being called to take part in his openness, share his suffering . . .

Voice 2 . . . with the promise of real glory to come – not just some sort of superficial jolliness!

Voice 1 Well, thank God for that!

A child lights the candle.

Minister This is the mystery we proclaim: Christ in us, the hope of glory!

All Thanks be to God. Amen

Minister We sing the first four verses of the Vigil Hymn. (See Appendix)

FIFTH SUNDAY IN LENT

Reader	Hear the word of God. Colossians 2:8-15
Voice 1	That's almost as complicated as last week's reading! What's all this stuff about 'circumcision' and 'uncircumcision'?
Voice 2	Well, circumcision was a kind of initiation, for baby boys, into the Jewish faith.
Voice 1	Oh, so in other words, it's about whether you're one of the crowd or not.
Voice 2	In a way, yes. St Paul says that we have been initiated into a whole new way of thinking. And it's so different from the old ways that it's like dying, and rising again to new life.
Voice 1	A new start. Yes, I can see that, but how does it happen? Where does the cross come in?
Voice 2	People used to think that they had to earn their way into God's favour – by keeping the laws, and so on. But because of the way Jesus died, we can see that God loves us in an amazing way, even when we do things that cause him terrible pain.
Voice 1	I can see that's a much better idea, but how does it actually help us?
Voice 2	Well, most children have had the experience of being desperately anxious to please their parents.
Voice 1	And . . ?
Voice 2	Can you remember how much better life was when you learned that you didn't have to do that?
Voice 1	I see what you mean – once we accept that, we're free to enjoy our relationship with them much more.
Voice 2	That's right. So, before we can even begin on any really meaningful relationship with God, we have to learn that about him.
Voice 1	I've got a feeling there's a lot more to it than that.
Voice 2	There is, but that's a start.
Reader	Hear the gospel of Christ. John 12:20-32
Voice 1	I knew there was more to it!
Voice 2	Living the way of Jesus will always be risky – and costly – but Jesus said it's eventually the way to life.
Voice 1	How does that happen?
Voice 2	Well, to take one simple example, if we stop trying to justify ourselves by being workaholics and take time to enjoy each other, we might be a lot happier.

Voice 1   But what if we *like* being workaholics, even though it might be destroying us?

Voice 2   I think you've made my point very well. But it is possible, because it doesn't depend only on us. We're back to the point about having the life of Christ within us. I don't say it makes it easy – nothing makes sacrifice easy – but it does make it *possible*.

Voice 1   Well, thank God for that!

A child lights the candle.

Minister   This is the mystery we proclaim: Christ in us, the hope of glory!

All   Thanks be to God. Amen.

Minister   We sing the first five verses of the Vigil Hymn. (See Appendix)

PALM SUNDAY

Reader	Hear the word of God. 1 Corinthians 1:18-25
Voice 1	I'm a bit puzzled.
Voice 2	Why's that?
Voice 1	Well, if God's got something against wisdom, why did he make life so complicated?
Voice 2	It's a good question. God isn't against wisdom – the bible often recommends it to us.
Voice 1	So, what's that all about? You said it was a good question, so how about an answer?
Voice 2	I'll have a go. The wisdom we're called to seek is the wisdom of God. The trouble is, we sometimes get above ourselves, and expect God to conform to our ideas.
Voice 1	In what way?
Voice 2	Most people think of God in terms of power – our kind of power, which normally means being destructive.
Voice 1	You mean, striking cathedrals with lightning, because he disapproves of the bishop?
Voice 2	That kind of thing. Tell me, would you try to bully your family into doing what you liked, or would you try to persuade them by love?
Voice 1	Ideally, by love, but it doesn't always work.
Voice 2	Not in the short term, but God's an idealist with time on his hands.
Voice 1	What do you mean by that?
Voice 2	Simply that God sees things in a different perspective from us, and often handles things differently from the way we expect. And he's prepared to take the time that's needed
Reader	Hear the gospel of Christ. Matthew 21:1-13
Voice 1	I've often thought it strange that Jesus didn't take advantage of all that people-power.
Voice 2	Perhaps he knew that in the long run it wouldn't accomplish his purpose.
Voice 1	Maybe, but what he actually did was upset some very important people. Now that was foolish!
Voice 2	And do you think that those crowds would really have supported him when the chips were finally down? In point of fact, it didn't take them long to change from a fan club to a lynch mob, did it?
Voice 1	That's true. Perhaps it wouldn't have been all that wise to do what they wanted, after all.

Voice 2   Fortunately for us, the 'foolishness' of God turns out to be better than our wisdom.

Voice 1   Well, thank God for that!

A child lights the candle.

Minister   This is the mystery we proclaim: Christ in us, the hope of glory!

All   Thanks be to God. Amen.

Minister   We sing the first six verses of the Vigil Hymn. (See Appendix)

Good Friday

Reader	Hear the word of God. Hebrews 4:14-16
Voice 1	I keep being told that the crucifixion changed the world, but it still looks pretty grim to me
Voice 2	It certainly wasn't an instant panacea for all evil, but it did open up an important new possibility.
Voice 1	What was that?
Voice 2	Well, tell me: when you're in trouble, what kind of person do you want to talk to?
Voice 1	Someone sympathetic, I suppose.
Voice 2	Right. So, if you had a choice between, on the one hand, a god who's spent his life sitting on a cloud, a long way from this world, and, on the other hand, a God who's actually been through what you are feeling, which would you feel most able to go to?
Voice 1	So that's what the cross is all about!
Voice 2	No – that's *part* of what the cross is about. But since we haven't got all day . . .
Voice 1	So it changes our ideas about God, and makes him more approachable.
Voice 2	Hopefully, although it's amazing how often we try to cling onto the old ideas.
Voice 1	Why do we do that?
Voice 2	Well, it's all very well in theory saying that the cross shows us a God who works by suffering love, by the power of persuasion, rather than by coercion, but in practice it's a bit harder than that.
Voice 1	Why's that?
Voice 2	Because if that's the way God works with people, it seems logical to deduce that it's also the way we should!
Voice 1	Trying to persuade, instead of bullying.
Voice 2	And being prepared to suffer, ourselves, in the process.
Reader	Hear the gospel of Christ. John 19:16-37
Voice 1	It really is a hard way of going about things!
Voice 2	But it's the only way that works, in the end. Openness to others, and being prepared to risk pain is God's way of doing things because he's wiser than we are.
Voice 1	But I'm not sure I can do that.
Voice 2	Comparatively few people ever have to, to the extent of the cross.

Voice 1	I don't think I could do it to any extent.
Voice 2	Well you're still a lot more confident than I am – because I'm quite sure I couldn't!
Voice 1	So, where does that leave us?
Voice 2	Back where we've been before: Christ in us, the hope of glory. Remember the christian idea about having the life of Christ within us – so we aren't asked to do it alone.
Voice 1	Well, thank God for that!
	A child lights the candle.
Minister	This is the mystery we proclaim: Christ in us, the hope of glory!
All	Thanks be to God. Amen.
Minister	We sing the Vigil Hymn. (See Appendix)

GOOD FRIDAY SERVICE

THIS service is not specifically related to the Lent Vigil, although with some adaptation to the order, it could be included. In those churches which have two services on Good Friday, the Lent Vigil could be incorporated in the morning service, and this order used in the evening.

The service is given in full-script form, which can be used with minimal preparation, or adapted as desired. Many ministers will probably want to re-word their parts in their own way, and that of course is quite legitimate, but the fully-scripted presentation may serve to ease the burden at this very busy time of the year.

The service explores the cross as an icon of the love offered by God to all creation, and of the suffering to which this exposes God. It consists of a series of hymns, readings, comments and meditations, all intended to help highlight particular aspects, as seen by the participants in the drama of Calvary. One person should co-ordinate the service and read the 'comments', the meditations being read by different people.

Order of Service

THEME OF THE SERVICE

> . . . you are precious in my sight, and honoured, and I love you.
> Isaiah 43:4a

OPENING SENTENCE

> Through the prophet Isaiah, God says to his people:
> > . . . you are precious in my sight, and honoured, and
> > I love you.
> Isaiah 43:4a

HYMN   O for a thousand tongues to sing
        or Praise to the holiest in the height

PRAYER OF APPROACH

> God of eternal love, we approach you with a sense of deep wonder. Your love reaches out to us in the face of rejection and pain. You suffer in the conflicts and failures which are our lives. And still you love us. Open our hearts and minds to contemplate the passion; assure us again of forgiveness and acceptance, and so fill us with your love that we may recognise and answer the call to share your passion in the world. This we ask, through him in whom your suffering love is revealed, Jesus Christ our Lord, Amen.

ASSURANCE OF PARDON

> But now thus says the Lord, he who created you, O Jacob, he who formed you, O Israel: Do not fear, for I have redeemed you; I have called you by name, you are mine . . . Because you are precious in my sight, and honoured, and I love you . . .
> Isaiah 43:1,4a

INTRODUCTION TO THE SERVICE

> What comfort can God offer in a world of pain? The stereotype images of God are quite unhelpful. A god who sits far above the world and pulls strings obviously does not care about our freedom; but a god who sits far above the world and does not pull strings clearly doesn't care at all.
>
> So how can a god be of any use to us?
>
> The christian revelation in Christ is that God does not sit above the world but involves himself in it, seeking to persuade, to influence, by relationship; – that he keeps that relationship open no matter what, and opens himself up to the pain which that entails – the same pain we all feel. God seeks to transform, not by pulling strings or throwing thunderbolts, but by the influence of his loving, suffering presence.
>
> This God is much harder to understand than the traditional stereotypes, and much of the time, he's harder to live with. But he's the only kind of God who makes sense in a mixed up world – and more importantly he's the God revealed to us in Jesus Christ – a God who loves us so passionately, so completely, that he cannot be apart from our pain. That is the God we shall seek to know just a little better this Good Friday.

We pick up the thread of the crucifixion story. Jesus has been arrested in the Garden of Gethsemane, and after a show trial has been convicted and taken to Calvary to be crucified.

READING   Luke 23:33-38

COMMENT:

'Father, forgive . . .' we hear those words so easily, and we forget how astonishing they must have been. I wonder what the reaction was of people who had been involved in the trial, and knew the whole context of those words. Let's hear from one of the soldiers.

MEDITATION (SOLDIER)

Yes, I drove in the nails. It's easy when you get used to it. I've done it so often that I don't need to think about it. I've grown so accustomed to the cries of pain that I don't even hear them any more. But this time it was different. This time I did hear something. Not the cries – it would take more than that to get through to me now. 'Father forgive . . .' Why did he have to say that? I can't forget it. It haunts me. He should have been angry – he should have howled for revenge. He should have called down curses on us all. What kind of man is he? Or, if he's who some people say he is, what kind of god is he? He's nothing like the gods I've been told about, that's for sure. We wouldn't have got away with doing this to them! Is it really possible that he is God? And if he is: is it really possible for God to love us – love me – that much?

HYMN   There's a wideness in God's mercy
          or And can it be

READING   Luke 23:39-43

COMMENT

Let us have no illusions over who this man was. We call him the penitent thief – actually, it would probably be more accurate to call him the penitent *revolutionary*. I wonder how he would have reacted.

MEDITATION (THE PENITENT REVOLUTIONARY)

I can hardly believe what I just said. I should despise this man: While some of us were risking our lives trying to do something positive to get rid of the Romans, he was talking about 'love' and 'forgiveness'. Why did I rush to his defence just now? There again, I can hardly believe what *he* just said, either. It's easy to talk about love and forgiveness, but this guy's actually doing it. Who is he? *What* is he? Is it possible to love the unlovable? Is it possible that, for him, nobody is unlovable?

HYMN   When I survey the wondrous cross
          or I know not why God's wondrous grace

READING   John 19: 23 -27

COMMENT

This is another dimension. I wonder how the 'Beloved disciple' heard this.

MEDITATION (THE 'BELOVED DISCIPLE')

Those other people might have been easier to forgive – he hadn't known them – they never promised him anything – they didn't owe him anything. But I did. I said I was his friend. We were special to each other – I always had the impression there was a particularly close friendship between us. He took me into his confidence when others were left out. We really did have something special . . . But when he needed me I wasn't there. Yesterday, he only asked us to stay awake and pray – that's all – and I couldn't even do that. When the trouble came, I ran away. So much for a 'special friendship'!

And now he's trusted me – me! – with his own mother!

HYMN   I cannot tell why he whom angels worshipped
             or O my Saviour, lifted

READING   Mark 15:33-39

COMMENT

'My God, my God, why have you forsaken me?'

Those words raise a vital question.

Did God, in Christ, really experience the whole human predicament, or did he just experience part of it? And could he truly be said to have experienced it if he went through this life with some kind of privileged information the rest of us don't have? God became fully human, with all that that implies. He had to live, as he calls us to live, by faith without proof. Only then could he say to us that he has experienced the human condition. Only then could he say to us that wherever we are, he has been there too.

So – what is the most terrifying of human experiences? Is it not to feel abandoned by God at the time of greatest need? That being the case, this cry of dereliction says that in Jesus God really was fully human. He knows the terrible feeling of abandonment, and he accepts the hurt we throw at him in those moments – because he has been there himself.

All that leaves very many questions still unanswered, because we are still left with a mystery. That's as it should be – whatever we say we still finish up with a mystery – the mystery of a loving and suffering God at the heart of human experiences.

HYMN   My song is love unknown
             or Jesus, lover of my soul

READING   Isaiah 43: 1-4a

COMMENT:

It's important to remember that the people to whom those words are addressed are not a particularly deserving group of puritanical saints. Far from it! They have disobeyed God, rebelled and blasphemed against him, worshipped other gods, killed his prophets, exploited the poor and oppressed the weak. And now they feel abandoned, in a strange country, cut off from God and deserted by him.

And it is to *those people* that he says:
' . . . you are precious in my sight, and honoured, and I love you.'

So we are left with an infinite mystery. A God whose power is made perfect in weakness – who contradicts all the worldly ideas about power and about justice. A God who is infinitely incomprehensible. But even with our dim understandings, we sense somehow that this is a God who is real – a God who is much more use to us than other gods are. We worship not a god – but God himself. Here's an expression of this mystery by Edward Shillito, who witnessed the carnage of the first world war, and found that a wounded God inspired him in a way no other could.

> The other gods were strong; but thou wast weak;
> They rode, but thou didst stumble to a throne;
> But to our wounds, only God's wounds can speak,
> And not a god has wounds, but thou alone.
> Edward Shillito: *Jesus of the Scars*

HYMN   Crown him with many crowns
or O sacred head

INTERCESSIONS

We pray with the crucified Jesus, for all who fear:
who fear   the loss of position
            the loss of security
            the undermining of faith

Father of the crucified, hear our prayer for all who are fearful, and who are moved by that fear to strike out at others, that they may learn the joy of letting go – letting go of all that burdens them, and holds them back, and taking the risk of love. May the cross of Jesus give them such assurance of your love that they may be free to love in return.

We pray with the crucified Jesus, for all who hate:

for fanatics for whom the cause has become more important than the people

for the victims of envy and those who nurse grudges

especially for all whose hatred is expressed in violence

Father of the crucified, we pray for those who hate, that they may find release in the experience of your love. May the cross of Jesus turn the energy of their hatred toward injustice and evil, that they may hate the things you hate, and love the world you love

We pray with the crucified Jesus, for all who are easily led:

Father of the crucified, we pray for all who cry for what they do not really want, and crucify hope; who are led into despair by malicious or foolish advisors; and those who are so desperate for hope or for love that they will follow anyone who seems to offer it.

May the cross of Jesus assure them that you will not abandon them, even when others do, and that they may safely be led in your way.

We pray with the crucified Jesus, for all who misunderstand:

Father of the crucified, we pray for all who look for a god of destructive power, rather than the power of love; for a god in the majesty of tinsel and fine clothes, rather than the majesty of faithful suffering:

May the cross of Jesus open their hearts and minds to a better knowledge of you, that they may find you in those places which seem least hopeful.

We pray with the crucified Jesus, for all who are bereaved.

Father of the crucified, you know the special agony of a bereft parent. And Jesus, in his own agony, found words for his mother and his friend. Look kindly on all who mourn, especially those who have lost their loved ones violently.

May the cross of Jesus lead them to find you in those places of deepest darkness which cannot be imagined but only experienced. And finding you may they know that their experience is yours, and be held in a love stronger than death itself.

In praying with the crucified Jesus, we find that we have been praying for ourselves. For we, too, often are fearful, or hateful, or easily led; we, too, seek a god made to our specifications, and reject you who offer so much more. We, too, know the pain of bereavement.

Father of the crucified, give us his strength and his love, that we may be his body on earth, and not fear to go into the darkness, there to be a light of hope for your people.

HYMN   Love Divine
          or Hail thou once-despised Jesus

CLOSING SENTENCE

Through the prophet Isaiah, God says to his people:
... you are precious in my sight, and
honoured, and I love you.
Isaiah 43:4a

BENEDICTION

Now go from here, in the knowledge and assurance of God's love,
and the blessing of God, Father, Son and Holy Spirit, be with you all.
Amen.

EASTER SERVICE

W E CELEBRATE the resurrection, not as past event but as present reality, and this service is designed to highlight the presence of the risen Christ in the world. It includes Holy Communion, as a celebration of that presence, in which the whole church takes part. Most christian traditions do not permit children to receive the elements, but seek other ways of including them in the service. Here, I have included an offertory procession, and also adapted the Passover practice, in which the children ask questions. There is, of course, no reason for restricting this idea to Easter, but at this time particularly it is surely right that we celebrate in as inclusive a way as we feel able.

ORDER OF SERVICE

As the congregation arrive, they are given tapers, or small hand-held candles (the latter must include either drip trays or holders). These will be used at the end of the service, when the light of Easter is spread symbolically through the congregation.

The Easter Candle is lit.

MINISTER   Alleluia! Christ is risen!

ALL   He is risen indeed! Alleluia!

HYMN   Jesus Christ is risen today
            or The day of resurrection

PRAYER

Holy God, we come to contemplate a mystery – to celebrate a truth which is deeper than mere fact. We come to proclaim resurrection, new life, as a gift from you. We come to worship and adore you. In the face of unspeakable mystery, all words and images fail; accept the silent worship which we now offer.

A Period of Silence

A LITANY OF THE RESURRECTION
(The whole congregation joins in the responses in bold type)

We confess, O Lord, that death is the great enemy in our lives.
So strong that it is hard to believe that Jesus is not buried in Palestine.
The angel said 'He is not here.'
'He has been raised again.'

We envy those who saw him face to face, and feel for Thomas in his doubt.
And yet we believe[7] he lives.
Jesus said 'Happy are those who never saw me'
'And yet have found faith'.

In the world we know we should be bold in the Master's service
but we find ourselves fearful and ill equipped.
Jesus said 'you will receive power'
'When the Holy Spirit comes upon you'.

We would prefer to be quiet christians. The responsibility of making Jesus known is a heavy one.
Jesus said 'You shall bear witness for me'
'To the ends of the earth'.

We are disciples of the Lord. We commit ourselves to his service and in his risen power resolve to make him known; by the way we live and by the words we speak. For overwhelming victory is ours through him who loved us, even Jesus Christ our Saviour. Amen.

Ian D. Bunting from *Prayers for Today's Church* by Dick Williams
(CPAS 1972)

---

[7]original: 'know'

THE CELEBRATION OF THE WORD

READING   Colossians 3:1-11

HYMN   Christ is risen! Hallelujah!
              or Come ye faithful, raise the strain

READING   Luke 24: 1-12

A CONVERSATION AT AN EMPTY GRAVE

INTRODUCTION

Where should we begin to look for the risen Christ? Over the centuries, millions of words, in various forms, must have been written about him, and they are very helpful. But they can no more contain him than the tomb could. In this dialogue, someone seeking Christ is directed first to words, but then to Christ himself.

Seeker   I'm looking for Christ.

'Angel'   Then what are you doing here?

Seeker   I heard he'd been killed.

'Angel'   Oh, that's yesterday's news! He's not here any more – he's alive. You'll have to look elsewhere.

Seeker   That's great! But where?

Helper 1   Now, there I can help you. The church has written down its beliefs in the Creed. Let me tell you what it says: 'I believe in one God . . .'

Seeker   Yes, I've heard that, and it was very helpful in telling me what I'm supposed to believe about Christ – but I didn't come away feeling I'd actually met him.

'Angel'   Christ is greater than any number of creeds. If you really want to find him, you'll need to look elsewhere.

Helper 2   I know where you'll find him. There's this wonderful song we learnt at church last week, and it tells you all about him – how he came from heaven, worked miracles, died and rose again. Let me sing it to you . . .

Seeker   Thank you, but I think I'll do without. I've heard lots of songs and hymns, and they really helped me to feel good taught me a lot about Christ, as well – but I still didn't feel I'd *met* him!

Helper 3   There's only one book where you'll find Christ. All the others may help, but the only one where you'll actually find him is the bible. Here – let me read you some of it?

Seeker   (Somewhat exasperated) Do you think I haven't read it until my eyes ache? It's done me a lot of good – it's because of the bible that I want to meet him. He's a really exciting person, according to the stories – but I've read them, and now I want to meet him!

'Angel'	That's fair enough. If you read the bible carefully, you'll find that it actually says that it's not the whole story[8]. And it also quotes Christ as saying that eternal life is in him as distinct from the scriptures[9].
Seeker	It's very nice to know that you agree with me, but it doesn't actually help me very much. Where do I look now?
'Angel'	Well, you've read the bible. It talks about people meeting the risen Christ in the ordinary things of life – while walking along a lonely road, or huddled in fear in a locked room. He himself said that wherever people are in need you'll find him.
Helper 1	Of course! It makes sense! The creed says that he became human, and shared our life and death . . .
Helper 2	And a lot of our songs and hymns are about his being with us in our lives . . .
Helper 3	And in Matthew 25, the bible says that whenever we help someone else, we meet him!
Seeker	So that's where we've got to go – out into the world among his people . . .
Helper 3	. . . and give help where there's need – then we'll meet him.
'Angel'	Yes, but don't forget the creeds, the worship songs, and, most of all, the bible.
Helper 1	You're a funny one – just a minute ago you were against all of those things.
'Angel'	No I was not! I just wanted you to get them in perspective, that's all. They all help us to find Christ – I just wanted you to understand that they don't actually contain him. Any more than the tomb could.
Hymn	He is not here, he has been raised. (See Appendix)

The Celebration of the Sacrament

The Offertory Minister

We offer our gifts of money, and with them we offer ourselves, all that we have and are. But the gospel is not one of works but of grace. So we remember Christ's own self-offering, placed before us today in bread and wine, and we join our offering with his.

Children lead the offertory procession, bearing bread and wine to the table. As they present them, they ask questions:[10]

[8]John 21:25

[9]John 5:39-40

[10]This adapts the traditional Passover practice, where the faith is explained through question and answer. The questions and answers given here are not intended to explore the depth of sacramental meaning. Rather, they give the children insight into one very basic aspect of it which children of most ages should be able to grasp. Of course, if this idea is used more regularly, different questions and/or answers can be substituted.

Child	Why is food shared in the service?
Adult	Because sharing food is a sign of friendship. It shows that we care for one another.
Child	What does the bread mean?
Adult	Bread represents life at its best. When we share it, we show that we are not selfishly keeping the good things for ourselves, but sharing them with each other.
Child	What does the wine mean?
Adult	Jesus spoke of suffering as a shared cup. It's easy to see how sharing one cup is a sign of sharing bad things. Sometimes being a real friend to someone can be risky. We show that we are willing to take the risks of friendship, as well as enjoy the benefits.

The offering of the congregation's gifts is received.

OFFERTORY PRAYER

God of resurrection, you offer us life; accept the lives we offer to you, represented by these small gifts, and transform them into signs of eternal hope, through Jesus Christ our Lord, Amen.

PRAYERS OF INTERCESSION

Minister   Here at this table we celebrate the presence of God in the world – in its pain and in its joy. It is therefore right that, around this table, we should enter into the pain and joy of the world, where God is. Let us pray.

We pray for all who are denied life in its fullness by the greed, fear or envy of others

Silence

Lord, in your mercy,
Hear our prayer.

We pray for all who have a vested interest in death, who keep the poor poor, and use terror to maintain their own positions

Silence

Lord, in your mercy,
Hear our prayer.

We pray for all who search for life at the tombs of this present world

Silence

Lord, in your mercy,
Hear our prayer.

We pray for all whose faith is stifled by over-dependence on written words, rather than the Word himself

Silence

Lord, in your mercy,
Hear our prayer.

We pray for all whose lives are overshadowed, and seem pointless

Silence

Lord, in your mercy,
Hear our prayer.

We give thanks for the communion of saints, the forgiveness of sins, and the life of the order to come. Amen

COMMUNION HYMN   Blest are you O God, Creator (See Appendix)
                  or And now, O Father, mindful of the love

INVITATION TO THE FEAST

Minister   Jesus said, 'I am not come to call the righteous, but
              sinners to repentance'.

All   Let us be brave, then, and approach God's throne where there is grace.

PRAYER OF THANKSGIVING

Holy God, we thank you for the splendour of the created order, and for humanity, created in your image, and crowned with glory and honour. In love, you have appointed us stewards and co-creators with you. We thank you especially for the perfection of creation in your Son Jesus Christ. In him you have shown us the full glory of your love, and the full glory of humanity, unfallen and unashamed. We thank you for his coming and living and dying in obedience to you, by the power of your Holy Spirit. We thank you that by that same power, he was raised to life, and by his life, death and resurrection opened the way to salvation, giving us a place in his perfect fellowship with you in the Holy Spirit. And now we call upon that same Spirit, that we may receive these elements of bread and wine as the body and blood of Christ. In union with the whole church on earth and in heaven, and as part of the great communion of saints, we fall silent before you in adoration and wonder.

After a brief silence, the prayer continues:

Holy God, coming to us in simple form, accept our thanks, and draw us more fully into the holiness and simplicity of resurrection life, through Jesus Christ our Lord, Amen.

WORDS OF INSTITUTION

*During these words, the bread is broken and the cup elevated,
in full view of the congregation*

For I received from the Lord what I also handed on to you, that the Lord Jesus on the night when he was betrayed took a loaf of bread, and when he had given thanks, he broke it and said, 'This is my body that is for you. Do this in remembrance of me.' In the same way he took the cup also, after supper, saying, 'This cup is the new covenant in my blood. Do this, as often as you drink it, in remembrance of me.' For as often as you eat this bread

and drink the cup, you proclaim the Lord's death until he comes.
1 Corinthians 11: 23 -26

A brief silence

SHARING OF BREAD AND WINE

PRAYER

Minister   Eternal God, we thank you that in welcoming us to your table
you have again assured us of your love for us, and enabled us to
experience it not only with our hearing, but by sight and touch,
and taste and smell.

All   Send us out, in the power of your Spirit to make our whole life
a sacrament of love, through Jesus Christ our Lord, Amen.

SPREADING THE LIGHT
*Some children light tapers from the Easter Candle and, from them, light the
congregation's tapers. (It is best to invite the congregation to find the next hymn
first, while they still have both hands free.)*

HYMN   Shine, Jesus, Shine
or Thine be the glory

BLESSING   Now let us go from here, in the power of the crucified
and risen Christ, to be signs of his life in the world.
And the blessing of God, Father, Son and Holy Spirit,
be with you all, evermore. Amen.

PENTECOST SERVICE

IF THE use of chants, such as the Invocation material used here, is unfamiliar to the congregation, it is worth taking time before the service begins to introduce them and briefly rehearse. If a solo singer who knows the chants is available to lead them, this helps break the ice.

ORDER OF SERVICE

CHANT	Come, Holy Spirit[11]
Minister	Let us, in silence, confess our sins to God.
	A short silence
CHANT	Have mercy on me, O Lord
READING	John 14:15-17
HYMN	Our blest Redeemer, ere he breathed *or* Come Holy Ghost, our souls inspire
READING	Acts 2:1-21

DIALOGUE

Voice 1	The sound of a rushing wind
Voice 2	Breath
Voice 1	Energy
Voice 2	Life
Voice 1	Filling the whole house
Voice 2	Every nook and cranny
Voice 1	Filling our bodies
Voice 2	Getting to the nucleus of every cell
Voice 1	Filling our lives
Voice 2	Every thought, word and action
Voice 1	Breath of life
Voice 2	Breath of freedom
Voice 1	Breath of God
Pause	
Voice 2	Tongues of Fire
Voice 1	Brightening
Voice 2	Burning
Voice 1	Consuming
Voice 2	Purifying
Voice 1	Transforming
Voice 2	Driving us out
Voice 1	Into the world
Voice 2	To offer life

---

[11]Chants used in this service are from *Invocation* by Colin Mawby, published by Kevin Mayhew, though of course spoken prayers of invocation and confession may be used instead.

Voice 1	Where there is death
Voice 2	Hope
Voice 1	Where there is despair
Voice 2	Burning, consuming love
Voice 1	Where there is cold, detached indifference
Voice 2	Come, Holy Spirit,
Voice 1	Like wind and like fire
Voice 2	Send us out
Voice 1	Transformed and inspired
Voice 2	Purified and enlivened
Voice 1	Signs of life
Voice 2	Signs of freedom
Voice 1	Signs of God

HYMN   Spirit of the living God
or Breathe on me, Breath of God

DIALOGUE *based on 1 Corinthians 12: 4-11, and 12:31-13:13*

Reader   Now there are varieties of gifts, but the same Spirit; and there are varieties of services, but the same Lord; and there are varieties of activities, but it is the same God who activates all of them in everyone. To each is given the manifestation of the Spirit for the common good. To one is given through the Spirit the utterance of wisdom, and to another the utterance of knowledge according to the same Spirit, to another faith by the same Spirit, to another gifts of healing by the one Spirit, to another the working of miracles, to another prophecy, to another the discernment of spirits, to another various kinds of tongues, to another the interpretation of tongues. All these are activated by one and the same Spirit, who allots to each one individually just as the Spirit chooses.
1 Corinthians 12:4-11

Voice 1	The gifts of the Spirit are given to individuals
Voice 2	For the benefit of all
Voice 1	One may have the gift of wisdom
Voice 2	Together we can learn that what is wise to God is foolish by human standards
Voice 1	One may have the gift of knowledge
Voice 2	Together we can know the love of God, revealed in the cross of Christ
Voice 1	One may have the gift of faith
Voice 2	Together we can show the love of God in our lives

Voice 1   One may have the gift of healing

Voice 2   Together we can help to dress the wounds of guilt, fear and oppression

Voice 1   One may have the gift of miracles

Voice 2   Together we can work the miracles of love

Voice 1   One may have the gift of discernment

Voice 2   Together we can learn to know what is good

Voice 1   One may have the gift of languages

Voice 2   Together we can learn the language of love and grace

Voice 1   One may have the gift of interpretation

Voice 2   Together we can learn to understand better what others are trying to say

Voice 1   There are many gifts

Voice 2   There is one Spirit

Reader   But strive for the greater gifts. And I will show you a still more excellent way. If I speak in the tongues of mortals and of angels, but do not have love, I am a noisy gong or a clanging cymbal. And if I have prophetic powers, and understand all mysteries and all knowledge, and if I have all faith, so as to remove mountains, but do not have love, I am nothing. If I give away all my possessions, and if I hand over my body so that I may boast, but do not have love, I gain nothing. Love is patient; love is kind; love is not envious or boastful or arrogant or rude. It does not insist on its own way; it is not irritable or resentful; it does not rejoice in wrongdoing, but rejoices in the truth. It bears all things, believes all things, hopes all things, endures all things. Love never ends. But as for prophecies, they will come to an end; as for tongues, they will cease; as for knowledge, it will come to an end. For we know only in part, and we prophesy only in part; but when the complete comes, the partial will come to an end. When I was a child, I spoke like a child, I thought like a child, I reasoned like a child; when I became an adult, I put an end to childish ways. For now we see in a mirror, dimly, but then we will see face to face. Now I know only in part; then I will know fully, even as I have been fully known. And now faith, hope, and love abide, these three; and the greatest of these is love.
1 Corinthians 12: 31-13:13

HYMN   Come, Holy Spirit, come! (See Appendix)
or Gracious Spirit, Holy Ghost.

PRAYERS OF INTERCESSION

Minister	Let us pray, mainly in silence, for the transforming power of the Holy Spirit in the world.
Silence	
Minister	Come, Holy Spirit
All	As transforming fire and life-giving breath
Minister	Let us pray for the transformation of ourselves
Silence	
Minister	Come, Holy Spirit
All	As transforming fire and life-giving breath
Minister	Let us pray for the transformation of the hearts of people of violence
Silence	
Minister	Come, Holy Spirit
All	As transforming fire and life-giving breath
Minister	Let us pray for the transformation of governments, that they may truly serve their people
Silence	
Minister	Come, Holy Spirit
All	As transforming fire and life-giving breath
Minister	Let us pray for the transformation of the ghettoes, in our cities and in our hearts, which separate race from race, class from class, person from person
Silence	
Minister	Come, Holy Spirit
All	As transforming fire and life-giving breath
Minister	Let us pray for the transformation of the church, that she may truly be a sign of vulnerable and suffering love
Silence	
Minister	Come, Holy Spirit
All	As transforming fire and life-giving breath
Minister	Let us pray for those we know who are in particular need
Silence	
Here, the congregation may be invited simply to mention names of specific people	
Minister	Come, Holy Spirit
All	As transforming fire and life-giving breath

Minister   Holy God, help us to live as those who believe
in the forgiveness of sins, the communion of saints,
and the transforming, life-giving power of the Holy Spirit,
through Jesus Christ our Lord, Amen.

OFFERING

HYMN   Come down O love divine
or I bind unto myself today

BENEDICTION

HARVEST FESTIVAL SERVICE

THE THEME of the service is Earth, Sea and Sky. The Old Testament writers knew that if we are to rely, as we must, on the earth to support us then we must take care of it. What is currently a fashionable issue (as distinct from one which is taken fully seriously) was for them a matter of responsibility and good stewardship.

So in this service, the congregation is invited to celebrate the planet's richness while acknowledging our responsibility. In its original form, the service was less scripted than here, and there is no reason why it should not be used in that form, where the resources exist. In the Earth, Sea and Sky section, the youth organisations of the church were asked each to provide a short item applicable to the theme, possibly presenting and explaining some object related to it. Some wonderfully creative things resulted, including at one point a host of 'CFC's (Brownies) rushing around the church, only to be zapped by some 'Ozone Friendlies'! If such participation can be arranged – and left largely to the creativity of those concerned, it will undoubtedly prove much better than the scripted version offered here.

The decoration of the church is of great importance. Let the imagination of the congregation be given full scope, so that the surroundings contribute to the service. There are many ways of reflecting the theme in the decoration. Were we the first church to include litter in its harvest displays, and to present a bag of it as part of the service? Perhaps we shall not be the last . . .

Order of Service

WELCOME AND EXPLANATION

The theme of the service is Earth, Sea and Sky. As we thank God for the produce of the earth, so we acknowledge our responsibility to care for it. We now recognise that conservation is not just for the professionals or the enthusiasts. We all have an interest in it, and a part to play. The decoration of the church reflects this, as do elements of the service.

HYMN   Come ye thankful people come
          or To thee O Lord our hearts we raise

PRAYER OF APPROACH

Holy God, Creator of all that is, we come to worship with a profound sense of wonder. We are only just beginning to recognise the vastness and the richness of your creation – only just beginning to realise the mystery of your being; a mystery which draws us, fascinates us, and as it does so, brings us to our knees in sheer adoration. We give you thanks for the hints of your glory to be found in creation, but even more for the revelation of yourself in Jesus, in whose perfect humanity divinity was at once revealed and veiled. Holy God, eternal mystery, open us again to the glory of your creation; draw us again into yourself, and as words and images fail us, open our hearts in silent wonder in your presence.

A brief silence

ACT OF CONFESSION

Let us now present before God the sins which spoil creation.
Let us confess the greed and the carelessness of which we are all guilty.

A bag of litter, collected from the surrounding streets, is brought forward.

PRAYER OF CONFESSION

Holy God, we confess our greed, our constant desire for more, our repeated cries of 'Bigger!' 'Faster!' 'Easier!' 'Richer!'. We recognise the harm which creation suffers at the hands of us who should be its stewards. We present to you the sins which threaten to choke your world; sins committed out of thoughtlessness, carelessness or ignorance, and the deliberate words and actions which spoil creation. Forgive us, and move our hearts to true repentance, that from this time on we may resolve, by your grace, to live more in harmony with the created order, through Jesus Christ our Lord, Amen.

ASSURANCE OF PARDON

Hear God's promise of forgiveness through the prophet Zechariah: 'I will remove the guilt of this land in a single day. On that day, says the Lord of hosts, you shall invite each other to come under your vine and fig tree.'
Zech. 3:9b-10

THE LORD'S PRAYER

OFFERING

including harvest gifts for distribution to the homeless, sick, housebound etc.

HYMN   We plough the fields and scatter
            or For the fruits of his creation

EARTH, SEA AND SKY

READING   Leviticus 25:1-7

A SECOND OFFERING
            Signs of good stewardship are offered by members of the congregation
            and their significance explained.

Presenter 1 Here is an aluminium can.
               Some people go through a great many of these in a year,
               and too often throw them away.
               They can be recycled and save the resources of the earth.

Minister   All creation belongs to God

All   Let us be faithful in our stewardship

Presenter 2 Here is a glass bottle.
               Some of the chemicals which pollute the oceans are by-products
               of the plastics industry. By buying products in glass bottles,
               where available, we can reduce pollution – and then recycle
               the bottle for good measure.

Minister   All creation belongs to God

All   Let us be faithful in our stewardship

Presenter 3 Here is a bicycle[12].
               One of the greatest pollutants of the air is the motor car,
               but pedal power, for those who are fit and able to use it,
               must be not only one of the cheapest but also one of
               the cleanest forms of energy. And it's good for you!

Minister   All creation belongs to God

All   Let us be faithful in our stewardship

Presenter 4 Here is an energy-efficient light bulb.
               Discharges from power stations have been held responsible
               for pollution of the air, the waterways and the land.
               Although expensive to buy, these bulbs last many times as long
               as conventional ones and use less power.
               So we can save money at the same time as saving the planet.

Minister   All creation belongs to God

All   Let us be faithful in our stewardship

HYMN   Harvest God, of life the giver (See Appendix)
            or God of concrete, God of steel.

READING   Matthew 23:23-28

---

[12]If space is limited, just a part – anything from a bell to wheel – could be used to represent the whole machine.

DIALOGUE

Voice 1	Now what on earth had that reading got to do with harvest?
Voice 2	Everything. Jesus was protesting about hypocrisy.
Voice 1	So what? He wasn't talking about harvest festivals, was he?
Voice 2	No, but he was talking about practising what we preach.
Voice 1	And?
Voice 2	Can you remember the response we've just used?
Voice 1	Course I can! Someone said, 'All creation belongs to God,' and we answered, 'Let us be faithful in our stewardship.'
Voice 2	Exactly. Well, words come easily to religious people. We always have more words than actions in our services.
Voice 1	Yes, and don't some of us know it!
Voice 2	So the real test of our faith is in actually living out, in the world, the things we've been talking and singing about.
Voice 1	Great! Now what's the next hymn?
Voice 2	Not so fast - there's more than that.
Voice 1	I should have known!
Voice 2	Jesus was really talking about justice
Voice 1	I remember – that stuff about 'justice, mercy and faith'. But how does that relate to a harvest festival service with a conservation theme?
Voice 2	Well, would you like the poor countries of the world to be as well off as we are?
Voice 1	Anyone would, wouldn't they?
Voice 2	And can you imagine what it would do to the environment, if they equalled our levels of consumption and pollution?
Voice 1	You're surely not going to say that they should stay poor, to save the earth for us?
Voice 2	You're right - I'm surely not going to say that. But that means that, if we're going to enable them to be better off, we've got to find cleaner and more economical ways of living – for ourselves and for them.
Voice 1	So, if we want to help stamp out poverty, all we've got to do is recycle our drinks cans, buy energy-efficient light bulbs and cycle to work?
Voice 2	Of course not. No-one suggests that it will cure all problems. We're going to have to accept much more painful and funda-mental changes in all our lifestyles. But conservation is part of the picture. And caring for God's creation means caring for all of it – we can't just pick out one bit and deal with it on its own.

Voice 1   So how will we finally get rid of poverty and injustice?

Voice 2   I don't know the answer to that. But I've got something here that will show us where to begin.

Voice 1   What's that?

Voice 2   *(Holding it up to the other's face)* A mirror.

HYMN   For the healing of the nations
or O thou who camest from above

PRAYERS OF INTERCESSION

We pray for creation and we re-commit ourselves to be co-creators with God.

Eternal God, we give you thanks for all you have created, and for the part you call us to play in the creative process. We pray that you will inspire us with your vision of creation, and motivate us to work unceasingly for peace, justice and harmony in every part of it.

We pray for those who are victims of the greed and shortsightedness of others. Especially we pray for those in the developing world whose products are swallowed up in an insatiable world economy while they are left to starve.

Silence

God of creation
Hear our prayer

We pray for nations at war, fighting over the earth's resources, or even the earth itself. We remember the victims of war, most often the very old, the very young, the weak and the sick.

Silence

God of creation
Hear our prayer

We pray for political leaders in the powerful nations of the world, that they may seek to pursue policies based on other-centred, rather than self-centred considerations, realising that wholeness in creation would be for our mutual benefit.

Silence

God of creation
Hear our prayer

We pray for the church, called to be a living sign of hope – to live visibly by radically different values from the world. We pray for courage and faith to withstand the pressures of society and thereby to proclaim life in all its abundance and simplicity.

Silence

God of creation
Hear our prayer

We pray for each other, and especially those in particular need . . .

Silence

God of creation
Hear our prayer

Finally, we give thanks, in faith, for the wholeness of creation, and reaffirm our belief in the forgiveness of sins, the communion of saints, and the order of the world to come. Amen.

HYMN   Now thank we all our God
              or Fair waved the golden corn

BENEDICTION

      Deep peace of the running wave to you
      Deep peace of the flowing air to you
      Deep peace of the quiet earth to you
      Deep peace of the shining stars to you
      Deep peace of the Son of Peace to you.

Remembrance Sunday Service

REMEMBRANCE Sunday is not an easy day for which to prepare. An increasing number of ministers are having problems with it, being sensitive to the genuine feelings of many in the congregations while holding profound doubts as to the value of the traditional approaches.

The problem, generally, is not the remembrance but much of what so often surrounds it. It must be right to remember; it has been wisely said that those who do not remember the past are condemned to re-live it. And to speak of war as a crime against humanity does not dishonour the dead. On the contrary; the most effective way of dishonouring those who die in war is to ask their sons and daughters to die after them, because the lessons have not been learnt. Let us truly honour the dead – all dead – of all wars, along with the wounded, the bereaved and the dispossessed – and we do it best by sincerely resolving not to repeat the sins which led to their suffering.

ORDER OF SERVICE

CALL TO WORSHIP

'Come, let us go up to the mountain of the Lord, to the house of the God of Jacob; that he may teach us his ways and that we may walk in his paths.' For out of Zion shall go forth instruction, and the word of the Lord from Jerusalem. He shall judge between many peoples, and shall arbitrate between strong nations far away; they shall beat their swords into plowshares, and their spears into pruning hooks; nation shall not lift up sword against nation, neither shall they learn war any more . . . For all the peoples walk, each in the name of its god, but we will walk in the name of the Lord our God forever and ever.
Micah 4:2-3,5

Silence

HYMN   Be still and know that I am God
or Creator of the earth and skies

PRAYER OF APPROACH

God of peace, you come to us in the noise and the conflict of our lives, to calm, to heal and to transform. Enable us now to worship you; to recognise your love, to wonder at the mystery of your being, and to rest on your eternal goodness, through Jesus Christ our Lord, Amen.

LITANY OF REMEMBRANCE

Minister   We remember, with honour, respect and repentance, all victims of war. We remember the dead:

A candle is lit by a member of the congregation

Voice 1   Past and present

Voice 2   Friend and enemy

All   We remember

Voice 1   Male and female

Voice 2   Young and old

All   We remember

Voice 1   Of all nations and races

Voice 2   Of all faiths and persuasions

All   We remember

Minister   We remember the bereaved:

A candle is lit by a member of the congregation

Voice 1   Husbands and wives

Voice 2   Sons and daughters

All   We remember

Voice 1   Friends and relatives

Voice 2   Lovers and dependants

All	We remember
Minister	We remember with sorrow the waste of skills and talents, hopes and dreams and of human lives with all their potential for glory.

A candle is lit by a member of the congregation

All	We remember, we grieve and we repent. God give us grace to honour those who died in war by living for peace. Amen.

OFFERING

OFFERTORY PRAYER

Holy God, we offer you our possessions, not other people's possessions; our lives, not other people's lives. We commit ourselves, not other people, to make sacrifices, in order that other people, not just ourselves, may live in peace and prosperity, and all creation enjoy the wholeness for which you allowed yourself to be broken. Amen.

READING   Psalm 46

HYMN   God of the nations (See appendix)
or Seek ye first the kingdom of God.

READING[13]   Matthew 6:9-13

READING

Our Father

'Our Father' says he: O hardened wretch! Can you call him Father when you are just going to cut your brother's throat? 'Hallowed be thy name' How can the name of God be more impiously hallowed than by mutual bloody murder among you, his sons? 'Thy kingdom come' Do you pray for the coming of his kingdom while you are endeavouring to establish an earthly despotism, by spilling the blood of God's sons and subjects? 'Thy will be done on earth as it is in heaven': his will in heaven is for peace but you are now meditating war. Dare you say to your Father in heaven, 'Give us this day our dailybread,' when you are going the next minute perhaps to burn up your brother's cornfields, and had rather lose the benefit of them yourself than suffer him to enjoy them unmolested? With what face can you say 'Forgive us our trespasses as we forgive them that trespass against us' when, so far from forgiving your own brother, you are going, with all the haste you can, to murder him in cold blood for an alleged trespass that, after all, is but imaginary? Do you presume to deprecate the danger of temptation, who, not without great danger to yourself, are doing all you can to force your brother into danger? Do you deserve to be delivered from evil, that is from the evil being, to whose impulse you submit yourself, and by whose spirit you are now guided, in contriving the greatest possible evil to your brother?

Erasmus

---

[13]The paired readings will be more effective if read by two people, on opposite sides of the church, the second of each pair being read without announcement.

HYMN   Dear Lord and Father of mankind

READING   Matthew 25: 31-46

READING

Whatsoever You Do

I was hungry and you fed the arms race to protect my 'freedom'
I was thirsty and you built armoured tanks instead of clean water tanks
I was homeless and you built fall-out shelters in your back gardens
I was naked and you clothed and trained the armed forces
I was sick but scientists were too busy perfecting new weapons systems
I was a prisoner of poverty and you argued that it was because of laziness,
or a necessary atonement for the sins of man

Then it will be the turn of the President and the Generals and all their supporters and all those who were indifferent to ask, 'Lord, when did we see you hungry or thirsty, homeless or naked, sick or in prison, and did not come to your help?' Then He will answer, 'I tell you most solemnly, in so far as you neglected to do this to one of the least of these, you neglected to do it to me.

HYMN   Jesus lover of my soul

DIALOGUE

Voice 1	You know, when I look around the world, and when I listen to the sort of stuff we've just been hearing, I wonder whether it's worth bothering.
Voice 2	Why's that?
Voice 1	Well, the world seems just to be going from one crisis to another, and the church is a long way from blameless in all of this. It just seems futile.
Voice 2	I agree it looks pretty bleak, but that's where the gospel of redemption comes in. In the end we're people of hope; we believe in God's future.
Voice 1	So we're supposed to put up with misery in the present because there's a wonderful future waiting – big deal!
Voice 2	No, that's not what it's about. The promise of perfect peace in the future protests against the present, and calls us to do something about it.
Voice 1	You mean, the fact that God wants a perfect world in the future shows how unhappy he is with the present one?
Voice 2	That's about it. In all of that, God is protesting – he's saying, 'This is what the world will be like, but just look at how it is now!'
Voice 1	So all that stuff about heaven isn't just supposed to keep people quiet?
Voice 2	On the contrary; it's supposed to make us angry, and motivate us to join the protest.

Voice 1   For a moment, there, I thought you were going to say,
'Join the revolution'!

Voice 2   Well, that's what it is! It's a revolution – a turning round –
of all our ideas about the way the world works.
And it's motivated a lot of people to begin working for change.

Voice 1   Like who?

Voice 2   Like Martin Luther King, for example.
The promise of the future made him angry about the present,
and he set out to change it. That's what real hope does – it
motivates us to change things.

READING   Revelation 21:1-7

READING

I have a dream

I have a dream that one day this nation will rise up and live out the true meaning of its creed: 'We hold these truths to be self-evident, that all men are created equal.' I have a dream that one day on the red hills of Georgia the sons of former slaves and the sons of former slave owners will be able to sit down together at the table of brotherhood. I have a dream that one day even the state of Mississippi, a desert state sweltering with the heat of injustice and oppression, will be transformed into an oasis of freedom and justice. I have a dream that my four little children will one day live in a nation where they will not be judged by the colour of their skin but by the content of their character.

I have a dream today.

I have a dream that one day the state of Alabama, whose governor's lips are presently dripping with the words of interposition and nullification, will one day be transformed into a situation where little black boys and black girls will be able to join hands with little white boys and white girls and walk together as sisters and brothers.

I have a dream today

I have a dream that one day every valley shall be exalted, every mountain and hill be made low, the rough places will be made plains, and the crooked places will be made straight, and the glory of the Lord shall be revealed, and all flesh shall see it together.

Martin Luther King

HYMN   We have a dream (See Appendix).

INTERCESSIONS

Let us honour those who have died in war, by joining our cries with theirs, that their sons and daughters will not be asked to repeat their sacrifice by a greedy and unappreciative world.

Silence

God of hope, to you we pray:
Stir us to anger, and bring us peace

Let us honour those who still die in war, by joining our cries with theirs, for a true peace based on justice and a proper sense of human dignity and worth.

Silence

God of hope, to you we pray:
Stir us to anger, and bring us peace

Let us honour those wounded in war, by joining our cries with theirs, for proper medical provision in times of war and of peace, and a true valuing of all human persons whatever their physical, mental or spiritual condition.

Silence

God of hope, to you we pray:
Stir us to anger, and bring us peace

Let us honour those dispossessed by war, by joining our cries with theirs, for a proper distribution of the world's wealth, for homes and the means of living with dignity.

Silence

God of hope, to you we pray:
Stir us to anger, and bring us peace

Let us honour those bereaved in war, by joining our cries with theirs, for adequate provision for the lonely and the orphans in our own society.

Silence

God of hope, to you we pray:
Stir us to anger, and bring us peace

Finally, in a few moments of silence, let us remember those of immediate concern to us (especially . . .)

Silence

Holy God, hear our prayer, and help us truly to live as people of faith, of hope and of peace, but above all as people of love, through Jesus Christ our Lord, Amen.

HYMN   God is working his purpose out
            or God of grace and God of glory

BENEDICTION

Go in peace to love and serve the Lord
In the name of Christ, Amen.

APPENDIX

Advent Carol

Tune: Noel Nouvelet

Hear the prophet calling; God is on the move,
challenging injustice with atoning love.
Grace comes with judgment; empires are destroyed;
captives liberated, victims overjoyed.

God would gladly give us all we really need;
do we want our freedom, or the chains of greed?
Grace comes with judgment, spirits to release,
and the Word disturbs us for the sake of peace.

Desert voices call us to prepare the way;
'Turn from sin and evil,' hear the prophet say.
Grace comes with judgment, words with passion burn,
calling us to listen, calling us to learn.

Wholeness in creation God will bring to birth,
joyously uplifting those of 'little worth'!
Grace comes with judgment, calls us to believe,
and in humble virtue, grace and truth conceive.

Topsy-turvy kingdom! Values upside down!
Baby in the manger cannot wear a crown.
Grace comes with judgment; God is in the straw,
homeless, weak and humble; let the proud adore!

LENT VIGIL HYMN

Tune: Picardy

Christ, who shared our human nature,
death's enslaving pow'r to break,
passing through this world triumphant,
tried and tested for our sake,
Christ in us the hope of glory,
all our failing lives remake.

By the presence of your Spirit,
give us wisdom to discern
truth from falsehood, good from evil,
and from all temptations turn.
Christ in us the hope of glory,
help us ways of peace to learn.

Now revealed among the nations
is the mys-te-ry profound:
All who freely share your passion
will in holy grace abound.
Christ in us the hope of glory,
life through death in you is found.

By your own life-giving Spirit,
let our lives transfigured be,
in your sovereign love rejoicing,
justified and fully free.
Christ in us the hope of glory,
be our light eternally.

Fullness of the Godly splendour,
now in weakness glorified;
fear of death by love defeated,
in the Word of life who died!
Christ in us the hope of glory,
crucify our worldly pride.

Now the shallow cries of 'glory'
stand revealed as verbal dross;
wisdom of the world defeated
by the folly of the cross!
Christ in us the hope of glory,
give us grace to share your loss.

Priest of all, once tried and tested,
free from evil and deceit,
giving all creation wholeness
by your wounded hands and feet;
Christ in us the hope of glory,
make your work in us complete.

HE IS NOT HERE

Tune: Rattlesden, in 'Thirty New Hymns'
published by Kevin Mayhew Ltd., or another L. M. tune

'He is not here; he has been raised;
why search the grave for one who lives?'
Such life the tomb cannot enclose
to all the world with joy he gives!

'He is not here,' the creeds confess;
no dogmas can his life contain,
but point us to the risen Lord
abroad in all the world again.

Our hymns and songs may lift our hearts,
but in the end will empty prove,
unless they turn us to the world
to seek his risen life and love.

The word in print, the scriptures say,
cannot the Word made flesh confine,
nor all the books in all the world
so well reveal the face divine!

Out in the world he will be found,
where deepest human need is known;
where sick are healed and hungry fed
and selfless, caring love is shown.

In darkened rooms; on lonely roads;
in shattered lives entombed in fear,
we hear the dancing Spirit cry,
'Rejoice, the risen Lord is here!'

Blest Are You, O God

Tune: Castlemaine. in 'Thirty New Hymns'
published by Kevin Mayhew Ltd., or another 87.87.D tune

Blest are you, O God, Creator;
through your goodness, bread we share,
by the earth conceived and given,
made by human skill and care.
Common food, by grace made holy,
bread of life to us will be.
Share we in the feast of heaven;
blest be God eternally!

Blest are you, O God, Creator;
by your grace we offer wine,
work of human hands combining
with the goodness of the vine:
cup of blessing, and of sorrow,
love's redeeming agony,
poured for us, our souls refreshing,
blest be God eternally!

Blest are you, O God, Creator:
Light of lights and Power of powers,
yet in humble love accepting
gifts from hands as poor as ours.
Love itself our love desiring,
O what awesome Mystery!
In our giving and receiving,
blest be God eternally!

COME, HOLY SPIRIT

Tune: Donnybrook, in 'Thirty New Hymns'
published by Kevin Mayhew Ltd., or another D.S.M. tune

Come, Holy Spirit, come!
Inflame our souls with love,
transforming every heart and home
with *wisdom* from above.
O let us not despise
the humble path Christ trod,
but choose, to shame the worldly-wise,
the foolishness of God.

All-knowing Spirit, prove
the poverty of pride,
by *knowledge* of the Father's love
in Jesus crucified.
And grant us *faith* to know
the glory of that sign,
and in our very lives to show
the marks of love divine.

Come with the gift to *heal*
the wounds of guilt and fear,
and to oppression's face reveal
the kingdom drawing near.
Where chaos longs to reign,
descend, O holy Dove,
and free us all to work again
the *miracles* of love.

Cont.

Spirit of truth, arise;
inspire the *prophet's* voice:
expose to scorn the tyrant's lies,
and bid the poor rejoice.
O Spirit, clear our sight,
all prejudice remove,
and help us to *discern* the right,
and covet only love.

Give us the *tongues* to speak,
in every time and place,
to rich and poor, to strong and weak,
the word of love and grace.
Enable us to hear
the words that others bring,
interpreting with open ear
the special song they sing.

Come, Holy Spirit, dance
within our hearts today,
our earth-bound spirits to entrance,
our mortal fears allay.
And teach us to desire,
all other things above,
that self-consuming holy fire,
the perfect gift of *love*!

HARVEST GOD, OF LIFE THE GIVER

Tune: Angel Voices

Harvest God, of life the giver,
hear the praise we sing,
you who fill both land and river
bless the gifts we bring;
gratitude but faintly spoken
through our token offering

For the skills of minds and fingers,
hear your people's praise.
Painters, poets, sculptors, singers;
each a tribute pays.
Thanks for all the skills of caring
and repairing, here we raise!

In our labours and our leisure,
may our praises show;
honest work and honest pleasure
both are seeds you sow.
For the joy of fruitful living,
our thanksgiving overflows.

Praise the God of triune glory,
Father, Spirit, Son,
Author of creation's story,
ever Three-in-One,
in whose blissful conversation
all creation was begun.

GOD OF THE NATIONS

Tune: Malvern, in 'Thirty New Hymns'
published by Kevin Mayhew Ltd.

God of the nations, hear our prayer;
from warring pride your people spare.
Let us in love and truth unite,
justice and peace be our delight.
God of the nations, hear our prayer.

Father, forgive the nations' rage:
prejudice passed from age to age;
banners made sacred, life made cheap;
widows and orphans left to weep.
God of the nations, hear our prayer.

Here may we glorify our dead,
building the peace for which they bled,
never to make their dying vain,
sending their sons to die again.
God of the nations, hear our prayer.

Teach us to turn our bombs to bread;
help us to see the hungry fed,
welcome the homeless, heal the lame,
freedom and hope for all proclaim.
God of the nations, hear our prayer.

God of the nations, hear our prayer;
from warring pride your people spare.
Let us in love and truth unite,
justice and peace be our delight.
God of the nations, hear our prayer.

WE HAVE A DREAM

Tune: Woodlands
Based on the famous speech of Martin Luther King
at the March in Washington on 28th of April 1963.

We have a dream: this nation will arise,
and truly live according to its creed
that all are equal in their Maker's eyes,
and none shall suffer through another's greed.

We have a dream that one day we shall see
a culture marked by what is just and good,
where children of the slaves and of the free
will share the common meal of brotherhood.

We have a dream of deserts brought to flower,
once made infertile by oppression's heat,
when love and truth annul the tyrant's power,
and streams of righteousness and justice meet!

We have a dream: our children will be free
from judgments based on colour or on race;
free to become whatever they may be
by their own choosing in the light of grace.

We have a dream that truth will overcome
the fear and anger of our present day;
that black and white will share a common home,
and hand in hand will walk the pilgrim way.

We have a dream: each valley will be raised,
and every mountain, every hill brought down;
then will creation echo perfect praise,
and share God's glory under freedom's crown!